# SPIDERS

CHAPTER I

Text: Maria Àngels Julivert
Illustrations: Marcel Socías Studios

Consulting Editor: Frederic L. Frye, DVM. MS, Fellow
Royal Society of Medicine

English translation © 1992 by Barron's Educational
Series, Inc.
Translated from the Spanish by Edith Wilson.

© Parramón Ediciones, S.A. 1991.

The title of the Spanish edition is *El fascinante mundo
de las arañas.*

*All inquiries should be addressed to:*
Barron's Educational Series, Inc.
250 Wireless Boulevard
Hauppauge, New York 11788

International Standard Book No. 0-8120-1377-8

Library of Congress Catalog Card No. 92-12257

**Library of Congress Cataloging-in-Publication Data**

Julivert, Maria Àngels.
    [Fascinante mundo de las arañas. English]
The fascinating world of spiders / by Maria Àngels
Julivert: illustrations by Marcel Socías; translated from
the Spanish by Edith Wilson.
        p.   cm.
    Translation of: El fascinante mundo de las arañas.
    Summary: An introduction to the physical character-
istics, habits, and natural environment of various kinds
of spiders.
    ISBN 0-8120-1377-8
    1. Spiders—Juvenile literature.   [1. Spiders.]
I. Socías, Marcel, ill.  II. Title.
QL452.2.J8513   1992
595.4'4—dc20                         92-12257
                                          CIP
                                          AC
Printed in Spain
2345     987654321

# SPIDERS

BARRON'S

# MANY THOUSANDS OF SPECIES

S piders are members of a class of animals called **arachnids**, which also includes scorpions, mites, sun or "wind" spiders, and harvestmen (or daddy longlegs). Of them all, the spiders—which belong to the order **Araneida**—are the largest group. There are about 35,000 known species in the world.

Many people dislike these arachnids because of their frightening looks. But the behavior of spiders is very interesting. Many of them weave astonishing webs with a skill and perfection that cannot be matched by any other animal.

The spider's body is divided into two parts: the **prosoma**, also called **cephalothorax**, and the **opisthosoma** or **abdomen**.

Spiders have an unusual pair of structures called **chelicerae**. These are found in front of their mouths. Each chelicera has a fang through which spiders inject their **venom** or poison.

At each side of the mouth are the **pedipalps**. They look like small legs but they serve as "feelers."

Only the arachnids have chelicerae and pedipalps, which they use to hold and crush their food.

Spiders have eight legs, which are attached to the prosoma. Each leg has two or three claws at the tip.

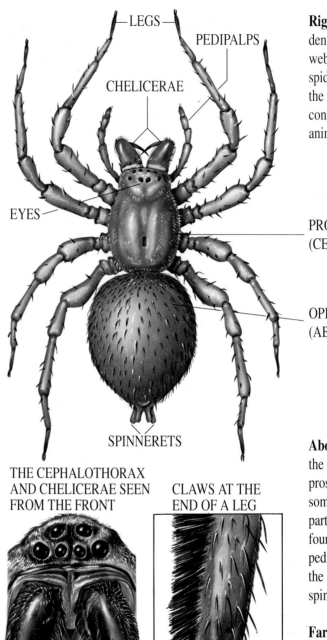

LEGS

PEDIPALPS

CHELICERAE

EYES

PROSOMA (CEPHALOTHORAX)

OPISTHOSOMA (ABDOMEN)

SPINNERETS

THE CEPHALOTHORAX AND CHELICERAE SEEN FROM THE FRONT

CLAWS AT THE END OF A LEG

**Right:** A common garden spider, sitting on its web. The webs of many spider species are among the most spectacular constructions made by animals.

**Above, left:** The body of the spider is divided into prosoma and opisthosoma. The other main parts of its anatomy are: four pairs of legs, the pedipalps, the chelicerae, the simple eyes, and the spinnerets.

**Far left:** The chelicerae are two small appendages found at either side of the mouth. Each ends in a hollow fang. Almost all spiders inject poison through these fangs.

# HOW DO SPIDERS SEE AND FEEL?

S piders have eyes and sensitive hairs that let them communicate and know what is happening around them. Through these organs, spiders sense movement and find their prey. Also, thanks to these sensory organs, the females can recognize the males during courtship.

Unlike insects, spiders have simple eyes. The number, size, and position depend on the particular species. Most of them have eight eyes, set in two rows, but some species have fewer eyes (six, four, or even two).

The majority of spiders do not have particularly good eyesight. Instead, these species have other senses that are highly developed. Some have an excellent sense of smell. But their greatest aid is a keen sense of touch. Spiders feel things through the many sensory hairs that cover their bodies and legs.

Many of these spiders are **sedentary spiders**—that is, they stay in one place and catch prey with the aid of an elaborate web. They know when an insect is trapped in their silky net by the vibrations carried through the threads.

Other species—sometimes called **wandering spiders**—catch prey by stalking and pouncing on it. To them, good eyesight is very important. Among them, the jumping spider has the best-developed sight.

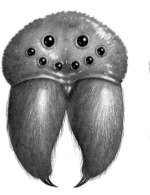

EIGHT SIMPLE EYES        SIX SIMPLE EYES

FOUR SIMPLE EYES        TWO SIMPLE EYES

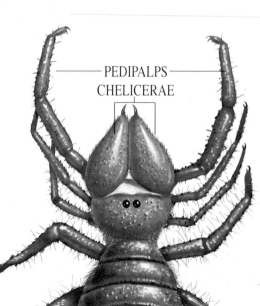

PEDIPALPS
CHELICERAE

**Above, left:** Spiders have simple eyes through which they can only distinguish intensities of the light. Most species have eight eyes, while others have six, four, or two; some don't have any!

**Below, left:** The hairs that cover the entire body are sensory organs. They are receptive to touch and allow the spider to sense temperature, humidity, and other things.

**Right:** These two spiders belong to different groups, which are distinguished by the way they live. The sedentary weaver, in the upper part of the illustration, constructs a web and has developed a keen sense of touch. The lower part of the illustration shows a jumping spider, which has highly developed eyesight.

# SILK MAKERS

Spiders have various silk glands with which they can produce several kinds of silk (dry, sticky, etc.), depending on what it will be used for. Silk comes from their glands as a heavy liquid. However, when spun into a fine thread, it becomes solid as soon as it comes into contact with the air.

The **spinnerets**, which are small openings located under the abdomen in the rear, discharge the silk. Spiders can have from two to eight spinnerets, but most of them have six. The size and location of these openings varies according to the species.

Silk is extremely important to spiders. They use it in many different ways.

Aside from its use in webs, silk helps spiders to move from one place to another. An anchored silk thread keeps them from falling to the ground. Female spiders form a silk case, or **cocoon**, around their eggs to protect them. Many species cover their underground shelters with silk threads and others even make various kinds of traps to catch their prey.

Although silk strands are extremely thin, they are very flexible and strong. A certain group, known as the **cribellate spiders**, makes a special type of silk that is sticky and blue in color. These spiders do not release the silk through the spinnerets but through a plate called the **cribellum**, which is found in the abdomen.

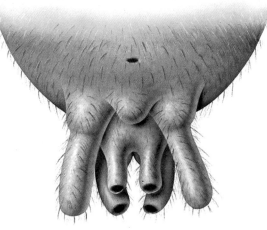

**A. CLOSE-UP VIEW OF THE SPINNERETS**

**B. THE CRIBELLUM**

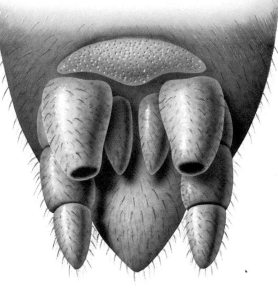

**Left:** The spinnerets (A) are the organs that contain the openings that release the silk secreted by the silk glands. Upon contact with the air, the thin strand of silk becomes solid. Spiders that have a cribellum (B) also have a set of hairs (C), called **comb**, for spinning the silk.

**Right:** Cribellate spiders expel the silk through openings in the cribellum ①, which is in the underside of the abdomen. These spiders make their spirals with an extremely sticky silk.②

THE HAIRS (COMB) THAT
CRIBELLATE SPIDERS
USE TO SPIN THE SILK

**C. ONE OF THE REAR LEGS**

# EXPERT WEAVERS

S piders create amazing constructions with thin strands of silk that they themselves produce.

Spider webs come in various shapes and sizes. The design of the web depends on the species.

Some species produce irregular webs, with the strands going in every which way. However, others, like the common garden spider, make perfectly geometrical forms.

This small arachnid weaves what is known as an **orb web**. Would you like to know how? After selecting a good location, the garden spider first attaches a few supporting strands to an object. It then forms a cross with several threads, known as radials. Finally, it weaves spiraling circles outward from the center. For the spirals, the spider uses a very sticky silk, so that insects will be caught and will stick to the web.

Spiders spin their webs in many different places—on a bush, in the bark of a tree, or even suspended between tree branches. They carefully tend their webs and promptly repair any damage.

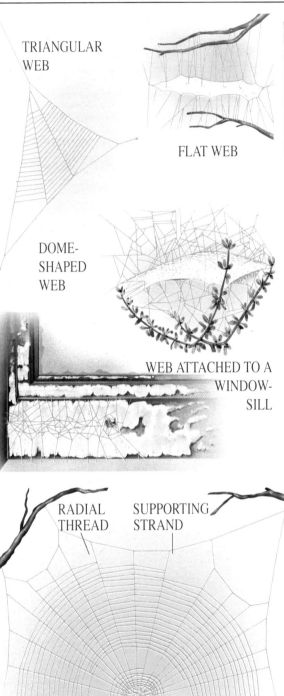

TRIANGULAR WEB

FLAT WEB

DOME-SHAPED WEB

WEB ATTACHED TO A WINDOW-SILL

RADIAL THREAD

SUPPORTING STRAND

CAPTURE ZONE

ORB WEB

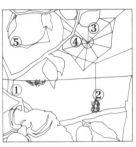

**Right:** Some spiders trap flying insects by means of a vertical web, usually placed between plants. Almost all vertical webs are started with a horizontal strand that the spider extends with help from the wind ①. Next, the spider moves to the center and drops down to add a vertical strand to the supporting structure ②. The radials follow ③. Now, the spider adds a spiral from the center out ④. When this spiral has dried, it will build another from the outside to the center ⑤, at the same time destroying the first spiral. The last spiral is made with a sticky silk that traps the prey.

# LOOKING FOR A MATE

**M**any spider species show **sexual dimorphism**—that is, males are different from females. Generally, males are smaller, have thinner legs, and are more colorful. The pedipalps of male spiders are different too. At the tip of each pedipalp, males have a special claw that they use to fertilize the female during mating.

Before looking for a mate, the male spins a small web and deposits on it a small drop of **sperm**, the liquid that the female's eggs need in order to develop. Later he will gather it with his pedipalps.

When they meet a female, male spiders behave in a special way. This behavior, known as **courtship display**, tells the female that the male wants to mate. The female then allows the male to approach her. Without the proper display, the female would confuse the male with prey and devour him.

The courtship display varies among the species. Some males do a complex dance, while others vibrate the female's web by softly tapping on the threads.

In some species, the male even resorts to tricks. For example, he may immobilize his partner with a few strands of silk, or distract her with an offering of food. Immediately after fertilizing the female, the male quickly leaves her side. If he is too slow in retreating, he can easily become his partner's next meal.

MALE AND FEMALE MATING

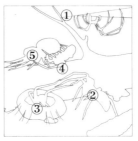

**Right:** On his sperm web, a male deposits a drop of sperm, which he later gathers with his pedipalps ①. This male ② is courting the female ③. He communicates with her by tapping his feet and pedipalps to avoid being devoured. Another male ④ immobilizes the female ⑤ by wrapping her in silk.

**Below:** Some species are sexually dimorphic, or distinctly different.

FEMALE

MALE

# CARE OF THE YOUNG SPIDERS

Spider eggs are round and measure only about ¹/₂₅ inch (1 millimeter) in diameter. The number of eggs in one batch varies according to the species—from 1 or 2 to more than 10,000 in the large species.

Spiders protect their eggs by bundling them up in a silk cocoon. Some species attach the small cocoon-like egg, or "brood" sac to the branches of vegetation. Others may conceal it among leaves or under a rock, then guard it from a nearby hiding place. Females of some species even fasten the sac to their spinnerets or chelicerae. Other females carry it on their backs or between their legs.

After some time, the eggs hatch and the tiny spiders emerge from the cocoon. Unlike insects, young spiders resemble adults, even though they are not completely formed at this stage. At this time they do not eat and stay practically motionless.

Soon they are able to feed. Now they look exactly like their parents, but smaller in size. Many females stay with their young for some time to continue protecting them.

The cycle of development from egg to adult varies in length, depending on the species. It is usually shorter in the smaller species.

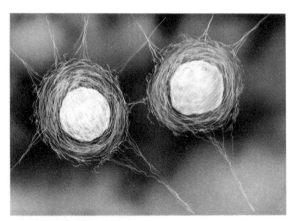

EGGS IN A SIMPLE CASE

Spiders secrete a special type of silk to protect their eggs. It may take the form of a simple ball of tangled silk or an elaborate cocoon.

**Right:** Many female spiders lay their eggs on plants ① or wrap them in a leaf ② for protection. Other spiders deposit their eggs in a nest ③. A few are devoted mothers who carry their eggs or young wherever they go—between their chelicerae ④ or on their abdomen ⑤.

EGGS IN A COCOON

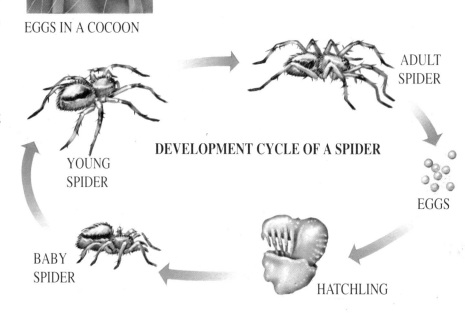

DEVELOPMENT CYCLE OF A SPIDER

ADULT SPIDER

YOUNG SPIDER

EGGS

BABY SPIDER

HATCHLING

# FLYING WITHOUT WINGS

In order to grow, young spiders need to shed or **molt** their outer skin several times until they reach adulthood. Under the hard **exoskeleton**, as this outer skin is called, a new one is formed. At first, it is flexible and lets the spiders grow a little before it hardens.

A few days before the molt, the spider stops eating. Web weavers hang upside down and push to split and slip out of their old skin. Once free, they hang by a silk line and stretch their legs to keep their flexibility.

Generally, smaller species need to molt fewer times than larger ones to reach their adult size.

At the last molt, they are fully grown. Many spiders no longer shed their skins after that. However, spiders that live more than one year may continue to molt to renew their exoskeletons, which may get damaged during that time.

Soon after birth, young spiders leave their nest to live alone. Some species let the wind carry them away. This method, called **ballooning**, lets them travel hundreds of miles in a short time. The young spider, while standing high on its legs, lifts its opisthosoma and sends a thin strand of silk up into the air. Like a balloon, the string is lifted higher and higher along with its passenger.

THE SPIDER HANGS UPSIDE DOWN TO MOLT

IT LOOSENS THE SKIN OF THE PROSOMA

IT RELEASES ITS OPISTHOMA

IT FREES ITS LEGS

**Right:** Spiders molt about five to ten times before they become adults. They hang upside down to free themselves from their old skins ①, but are safely suspended by a strand of silk. After the first few molts, the young spiders disperse. Climbing to the top of a plant, they lift their abdomen ② and let the wind transport them while attached to a silk thread ③.

WANDERING SPIDERS MOLT THEIR EXOSKELETONS ON THE GROUND

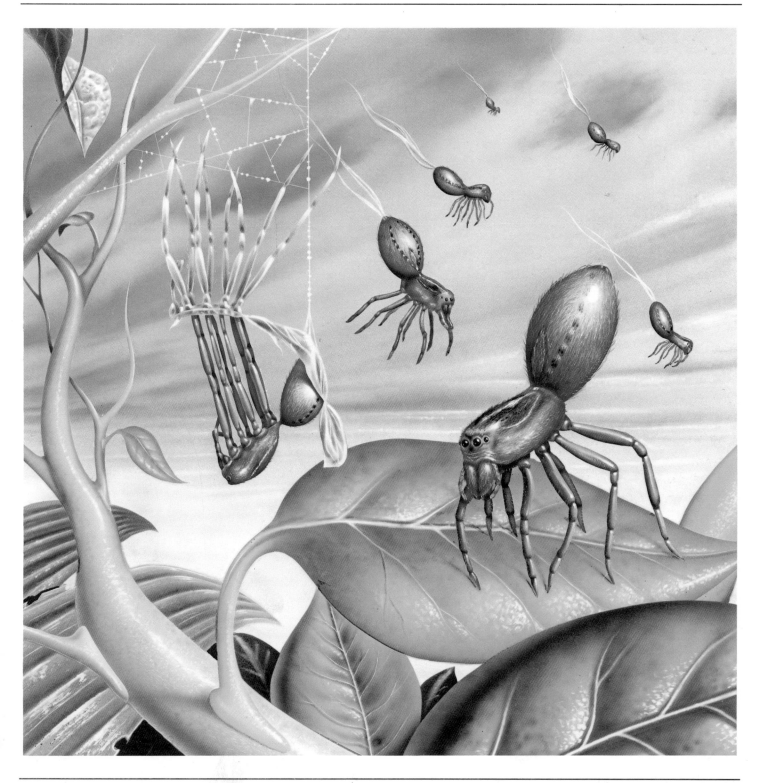

# GREAT HUNTERS

**S**piders are great hunters. They feed mostly on insects, such as bees, wasps, beetles, grasshoppers, and others. A few of the larger species may even capture small rodents and birds.

Upon catching its prey, the spider sprays or injects it with a fluid that digests the prey and turns it into liquid, which the spider can then suck up.

Hunting methods vary from species to species. Wandering spiders, for example, pounce upon their prey and inject them with venom. By contrast, other spiders spin webs to trap flying insects. In its attempts to free itself, the prey vibrates the threads. The movement alerts the waiting spider, which immediately responds by wrapping its prey in a sticky silk. The prey is then injected with venom.

Some species even try to look and act like their prey. For example, certain ant-eating spiders have adapted their bodies to look like ants. This allows them to approach ants without alarming them.

Crab spiders do not spin webs: they use **camouflage**. Their colors blend with the colors of the plants that they live on making them practically unnoticeable. They remain very still and patiently wait for an unsuspecting insect to appear. When it does, they pounce on it, immobilizing it with their venom.

**A**

RED ANT

ANT-EATING SPIDER

**B**

**Right:** Weavers ① know when prey ② is trapped in their web by sensing the vibrations. The spider makes sure it will receive the signals by adding many radial threads that meet at the center of the web. There the spider waits in ambush. If the prey is too large, the spider hides. When prey is the "right" size, the spider wraps it in a sticky silk ③.

**Above and right:** Hunting methods vary among species of wandering spiders: They imitate ants (A), lie in ambush at their nest's entrance (B), or actively search for prey, which they paralyze with venom (C).

**C**

# POISONOUS SPIDERS

With a few exceptions, all spiders have poison. The poison glands are located at the base of the chelicerae and open into a duct that reaches down to the fangs.

The power of the poison depends on the spider species and on the size of the prey receiving the poison. It is usually deadly for other spiders, insects, small mammals, birds, and reptiles.

Of course, the size of the spider is also important. A large spider is easily able to pierce the skin of a small animal and inject a larger amount of poison.

Of the many spiders that exist, only a few are harmful to humans. The chelicerae of most spiders are not strong enough to penetrate human skin: In addition, the poison of many species is too weak to be harmful to people.

Some spiders are extremely dangerous, like the black widow. Although this spider is small, its poison can cause death in humans.

The most poisonous and aggressive spiders are from South America. The banana spider is widely feared. Its bite is deadly. Most of the tarantulas, despite their bad reputation, are not actually very dangerous.

POISON GLAND     CHELICERA     FANG

**Left:** Poison is released from a gland located in the chelicera and travels out through the fangs. The poison's effectiveness depends on the size of the prey and on the species and size of the spider.

**Right:** Few spider species are harmful to humans. Among the most notorious is the black widow. Here you can see it climbing along a plant stem, hunting among the leaves, and hanging upside down in its web.

# DIVING SPIDERS

Spiders breathe through either of two types of organs: **book lungs** or **tracheae**. However, a few species have both. The respiratory openings are located on the underside of the abdomen.

Most spiders live on land, but some species live near water and are even able to walk on the water's surface. In case of danger, they may sometimes dive by holding onto submerged plants.

One of the very few true aquatic species is *Argyroneta aquatica*, which lives, hunts, feeds, and reproduces under water. However, like all spiders, it needs to breathe air. Then how can it spend most of its life under water?

This small spider is an expert diver and builds an underwater shelter. It weaves a fine silken cloth-like web, which it attaches to underwater plants. The spider then fills the cloth with air to form a bell-like chamber, which has an opening underneath to admit the spider. As the supply of air is used up, the water spider refills it.

When leaving the bell to hunt, the spider takes with it a small bubble of air attached to its abdomen. This allows it to breathe. The water spider is a good swimmer who feeds on small fish.

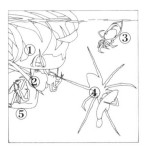

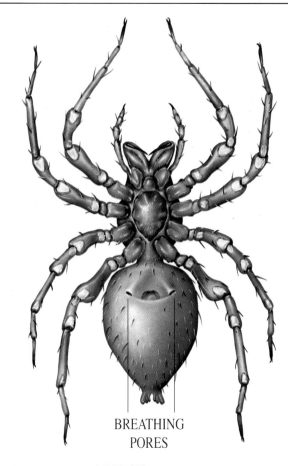

BREATHING
PORES

SPIDER ADAPTED FOR WALKING
ON WATER

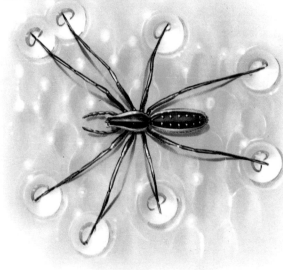

**Above, left:** The openings for breathing are located on the underside of the abdomen.

**Below, left:** Some water spiders are able to walk on the water's surface.

**Right:** *Argyroneta aquatica* weaves a silky cloth between the submerged plants of certain rivers ①. It then fills the cloth with air bubbles ② carried from the surface ③. This spider captures insects and fish and injects them with venom ④. It can breathe under water because its unusual home holds a supply of air ⑤.

# UNDERGROUND ARCHITECTS

Certain spiders dig burrows in the ground. These subterranean homes may consist of one or more tunnels. Their shape varies according to the species.

These spiders spend the greater part of their live's inside their burrows. From time to time they emerge to hunt for prey.

Only the males leave the burrow in search of a mate during the reproductive season.

Trapdoor spiders dig a tubular tunnel and line its walls with silk. They then construct a door, called an **operculum**, to camouflage the entrance. This door is attached to the tunnel opening on one side. The spider can open and close it at will.

When an insect passes by its lair, the spider quickly opens the hinged door to capture it. If danger threatens, the spider shuts the door making it difficult to detect.

Some cribellate spiders also live in silk-lined burrows, but do not construct doors. Instead, they install a silken tube that rises above the entrance. The spider camouflages this tube with dirt and plant litter.

## NEST OF A SPIDER OF THE GENUS *NEMESIA*

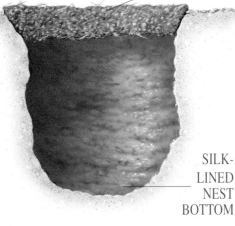

OPERCULUM

SILK-LINED NEST BOTTOM

## NEST OF A CRIBELLATE SPIDER

TUNNEL ENTRANCE COVERED WITH SILK AND PLANT LITTER

**Above , left:** Nest built by a spider of the genus *Nemesia*, with its entrance covered by a door.

**Below, left:** Nest of a cribellate spider, without a door.

**Right:** Some spiders make their nests below ground. These shelters not only keep their babies safe, but also make hunting easier. Although they occasionally go hunting away from the nest ①, the well-camouflaged doorway ② makes it easier for them to surprise an unwary prey by lying in wait at home ③.

# LIFE IN A COMMUNITY

Spiders are eager predators, so it is not unusual for them to attack one another. For this reason, most of them prefer a solitary life. Only during the first part of their development do spiders group together. However, they soon separate to become independent.

A few cases of sociable or **gregarious** spiders exist, but their organization is not as perfect as that of bees or ants.

Some species merely tolerate one another. Though they live close together, each has its own web. Others go a little further—they hunt in groups and share the catch with all members of the community.

More complex social systems include spiders that spend their entire lives together in one large web. They form colonies of more than one hundred individuals. The members do everything as a group. They hunt, eat, and reproduce together, but they still lay their eggs in individual egg sacs.

On the American continent there are various spider species that sometimes gather in groups. Community life is most useful at hunting time.

COMMUNITY NEST

PREY CAUGHT IN A COMMUNITY WEB

**Left:** Some species form a society and live together in a large web.

**Below:** When prey is trapped in a community web, all the spiders in the colony surround it.

**Right:** Most spiders wrap their eggs in individual cocoons, but the females of this Mexican species each deposit two or three eggs in the same egg sac. Their young all develop together in the community's nursery web.

# SPIDERS CAN LOSE THEIR LEGS AT WILL

Spiders are good for the environment because they control insect populations by eating them. Of course, spiders are preyed upon, too. Small mammals, birds, frogs, some insects, and even others of their own kind—eat spiders.

When faced with an enemy, most spiders choose to flee. They sometimes let themselves fall, attached to a silk thread, which they use for climbing back up when danger has passed.

Some species trick their enemies by pretending to be dead. When threatened, they fall to the ground, curl their legs tightly under their bodies, and stay motionless.

When necessary, many spiders are able to lose any of their legs voluntarily. This strange phenomenon, known as **autotomy**, often allows them to escape their predators.

The leg always breaks off at the same joint. During the next molt it will grow back, although the new leg is usually shorter and thinner than the original one.

After the last molt occurs, however, the spider is no longer able to replace a lost limb.

**Left:** This spider uses camouflage as a protective device.

**Below:** Dropping a leg is a defense technique that misleads its enemies. The limb grows back if the spider has not completed its final molt.

**Right:** To avoid ending up in the mouth of a frog ①, the other spiders shown here use various defense techniques. One escapes by climbing up its silk strand ②, another drops a leg to confuse the predator ③, and the other plays dead ④. However, the chief danger to small spiders comes from the large spiders ⑤.

# Glossary

**abdomen.** See *opisthosoma*.

**arachnids.** Class of animals that breathe air, have four pairs of legs, and a body consisting of two or more segments. For example, spiders, harvestmen (daddy longlegs), scorpions, mites, and others.

**Araneida.** Order that includes all spiders.

**autotomy.** Ability that some animals have to remove some part of their body at will. In the case of the spiders, they detach their legs.

**ballooning.** Method used by young spiders to separate from their brothers and sisters. The ballooning spider flies through the air attached to a long silken thread, which is spun to catch the wind.

**book lungs.** One of two types of respiratory organs of the arachnids. Organ has folds of tissue resembling the pages of a book. See also *tracheae*.

**camouflage.** Method of blending with surrounding colors to become practically unnoticeable.

**cephalothorax.** See *prosoma*.

**chelicerae.** First pair of structures arachnids have at each side of the mouth with which they capture and crush their prey.

**cocoon.** Silk case formed by spiders to protect their eggs.

**comb.** Special hairs on the rear legs of cribellate spiders. (See *cribellum*.) Comb is used in the spinning of silk.

**cribellate spiders.** A group of spiders that make a type of blue silk that is quite sticky.

**cribellum.** Organ that secretes a special kind of silk. In some spiders the cribellum is found in front of the spinnerets.

**exoskeleton.** Hard outside structure that supports the body of spiders and other animals.

**gregarious.** Referring to spiders or other animals who live together as a group.

**molt.** Act of shedding an external part of the body. It is usually followed by replacement of the discarded parts.

**operculum.** Lid or door constructed of silk and soil that certain spiders use to seal off the entrance of their shelters.

**opisthosoma.** Rear part of the spider body; also called *abdomen*.

**pedipalps.** Second pair of appendages that spiders have between the chelicerae and legs.

**prosoma.** Front part of the spider body; also called *cephalothorax*.

**sedentary spiders.** Group of spiders that will live out their lives in one place when left undisturbed. Most of them spin webs to trap flying insects. (Contrast with *wandering spiders*.)

**sexual dimorphism.** Difference in size, color, or shape, between the male and female of the same species.

**sperm.** The special male cells needed for the reproduction of a species.

**spinnerets.** Organs of spiders used for spinning the silk produced in the silk glands.

**tracheae.** Respiratory tubes of the arachnids. Some spiders have this type of organ as well as another more primitive type. See *book lungs*.

**venom.** Poison, injected through the spider's fang, used to paralyze prey.

**wandering spiders.** Spiders that have adapted to an active life without the orb web. Some, such as the jumping spider, have highly developed eyesight. (Contrast with *sedentary spiders*.)

# Index